21st
Century
Skills Library

REAL WORLD MATH: GEOGRAPHY

CONTINENTS

BY ANN HEINRICHS

CHERRY
LAKE
Publishing

Published in the United States of America by
Cherry Lake Publishing, Ann Arbor, Michigan
www.cherrylakepublishing.com

Content Adviser
Andrew Dombard, PhD, Associate Professor, Department of Earth and Environmental
Sciences, University of Illinois at Chicago
Math Adviser: Tonya Walker, MA, Boston University

Credits
Photos: Page 4, ©iStockphoto.com/solarseven; page 6, ©Melissa Dockstader, used
under license from Shutterstock, Inc.; page 8, ©Gary718/Dreamstime.com; page 11,
©iStockphoto.com/fanelliphotography; page 13, ©JUPITERIMAGES/STOCK IMAGE/
Alamy; page 14, ©Inspe/Dreamstime.com; page 16, ©Robert Kyllo, used under
license from Shutterstock, Inc.; page 19, ©iStockphoto.com/Alfsky; page 20,
©Friedrich Saurer/Alamy; page 23, ©Rob Cousins/Alamy; page 25, ©Dennis Hallinan/
Alamy; page 26, ©Pichugin Dmitry, used under license from Shutterstock, Inc.

Library of Congress Cataloging-in-Publication Data
Heinrichs, Ann.
  Continents / by Ann Heinrichs.
      p. cm.—(Real world math: geography)
  Includes index.
  ISBN-13: 978-1-60279-490-0
  ISBN-10: 1-60279-490-1
  1. Continents—Juvenile literature. I. Title. II. Series.
  G133.H45 2010
  910.914'1—dc22   2008052360

Cherry Lake Publishing would like to acknowledge
the work of The Partnership for 21st Century Skills.
Please visit *www.21stcenturyskills.org* for more information.

TABLE OF CONTENTS

CHAPTER ONE
WHERE IN THE WORLD ARE YOU?

A giraffe nibbles on leaves from a tree, while elephants graze in the background. Where in the world are you? You're in Africa!

Penguins waddle across the ice as seals splash in the freezing cold waters. Where in the world are you now? Antarctica!

More than 60 different kinds of kangaroos live in Australia. They live in all parts of the continent.

Kangaroos bound across the plains, while cuddly koalas cling to tree trunks. Where are you this time? Australia!

Africa, Antarctica, and Australia are all continents. Continents are Earth's large landmasses. There are seven continents: Africa, Antarctica, Asia, Australia, Europe, North America, and South America. When you study continents, you'll find that math plays a big part in your studies. Just counting the continents is trickier than you might think.

In general, the continents are separated by large bodies of water. For example, the Pacific Ocean lies between Asia and North America. But some continents are connected to each other. Europe and Asia share a border that is hundreds of miles long. Other continents are joined by a small strip of water or land. So how did we end up counting seven continents? Over the years, people have looked at many factors when defining continents. They've looked at things such as an area's history, culture, and population. These things strongly unite the regions. So the number seven became accepted over time.

Continents vary in size, shape, weather, and culture. Many things make each continent different from the others.

REAL WORLD MATH CHALLENGE

Asia covers about 17 million square miles. Australia covers about 3 million square miles. **How many Australias would fit inside Asia?**

(Turn to page 29 for the answer)

In size, the largest continent is Asia. It is followed by Africa, North America, South America, Antarctica, and Europe. Australia, home of the kangaroos, is the smallest of the seven continents.

Most continents are divided into countries, which have their own governments. Africa has the most countries, with 53. Europe has about 46 countries. Asia has about 44, depending on what counts as a country. North America is made up of 23 countries. The three largest are Canada, the United States, and Mexico. South America has 12 countries.

Australia is both a continent and a country. But Antarctica is not a country at all. It surrounds the South Pole, and 98 percent of the continent is ice. Antarctica doesn't belong to any country, and no one lives there. Some scientists spend time on Antarctica doing research, but no one considers it home. No one except the penguins, that is!

CHAPTER TWO

HEMISPHERES, SEASONS, AND DAYS

One way of studying the continents is to look at hemispheres. *Hemisphere* means "half a sphere," or half of a ball-shaped object. Since Earth is a sphere, it can be divided into hemispheres. For the Northern and Southern

Montreal 73° 34' W
Ottawa 75° 43' W
Chicago 87° 45' W
New York 73° 50' W
Madrid 3° 43' W
Washington
Lisbon

Rome 12° 30' E
Istanbul 28° 57'
Beijing 116° 25'
Athens 23° 44'
Seoul 127° 00'
Tokyo 139° 45'

This is a marker placed where the prime meridian passes through Greenwich. It lists locations of cities as measured from this line.

Hemispheres, the dividing line is the equator. That's an imaginary line running in an east–west direction around the center of Earth.

Most of Earth's land lies in the Northern Hemisphere. Europe and North America are in the Northern Hemisphere. So are almost all of Asia and about two-thirds of Africa. In the Southern Hemisphere are the continents of Australia and Antarctica. Most of South America and about one-third of Africa are in the Southern Hemisphere, too.

Earth can also be divided into Eastern and Western Hemispheres. In this case, the dividing line is the **prime meridian**. This is an imaginary north–south line that passes through Greenwich, a section of London, England. The half of Earth lying east of this line is the Eastern Hemisphere. Lands to the west are in the Western Hemisphere.

Dividing the world this way, most of Earth's land is in the Eastern Hemisphere. Most of Europe and Africa and all of Asia and Australia are in the Eastern Hemisphere. The only continents completely within the Western Hemisphere are North America and South America.

Once you understand hemispheres, you can learn a lot about life on other continents. Take the seasons, for example. Earth spends one year revolving around the Sun. Because Earth is slightly tilted as it revolves, sometimes one hemisphere is tipped closer to the Sun than the other

LIFE & CAREER SKILLS

Melbourne, Australia, hosted the Summer Olympics in 1956. This was the first time the Olympics were held in the Southern Hemisphere. Many members of the International Olympic Committee were not sure Melbourne would be a good location for summer games. Events would be held in November and December, just as Australia's summer was beginning. But many athletes were coming from the Northern Hemisphere. This would be winter for them, and they were used to resting during the winter. Instead, they would have to reach their peak performance at this time of year. Athletes had to adjust their training habits to prepare for the Olympics in Melbourne.

hemisphere. During one quarter of the year, the Northern Hemisphere is tilted toward the Sun, while the Southern Hemisphere is tilted away. This brings summer to the Northern Hemisphere and winter to the Southern Hemisphere. Six months later the situation is reversed. The North tilts away and the South tilts toward the Sun, making northern lands

The Sun shines longer on the hemisphere tilted toward it. More time in the sun means warmer air, which creates summer.

chilly and southern lands warm. In between are seasons of transition, either spring or fall.

Your time of day is related to your hemisphere, too. Day and night happen as Earth rotates on its axis. Earth makes a full rotation in 24 hours. When one side of Earth faces the Sun, the opposite side faces away from the Sun. Suppose it's 3:00 P.M. in Toronto, Canada. That's in North America, in the Western Hemisphere. At the same time, it's 3:00 A.M. in Bangkok, Thailand. That's in Asia, in the Eastern Hemisphere. People there are fast asleep. If you live in Toronto, 3:00 P.M is not a good time for a friendly phone call to Bangkok!

REAL WORLD MATH CHALLENGE

On Christmas Day (December 25) in Australia, many people are going to the beach. Exactly 6 months later, they're shivering. On that same day, while Australians are shivering, people in Kansas are looking forward to Independence Day. **What day is it? How many more days do people in Kansas have to wait for Independence Day?**

(Turn to page 29 for the answers)

Christmas is a summer holiday in Australia.

CHAPTER THREE
DO THE MATH: USING MAP SCALES

Your big, fluffy cat stretches out on your desk. The cat is 24 inches (61 centimeters) long, from its nose to the tip of its tail. Now you draw a picture of your cat. You can't draw its full

Maps help people find their way. Using a map scale, they can find out the distance between two points.

size. That's bigger than your piece of paper! Instead, you draw a cat that's only 6 inches (15.2 cm) long. With a 24-inch cat and a 6-inch picture, you drew the cat at one-fourth of its full size. That's called drawing on a scale of 1 to 4. Your picture still looks like the cat, only it appears on a smaller scale.

Maps are drawn the same way. The whole world could never fit on a piece of paper. That's why maps are drawn on a smaller scale. Looking at maps, people can visualize lands that are too large or far away to see with their eyes.

LEARNING & INNOVATION SKILLS

Using maps, you find the shortest distance between two points. However, the driving distance between those points can be much longer. For example, on a map, it's 316 miles (509 kilometers) from Frankfurt, Germany, to Milan, Italy. However, the driving distance between the two cities is about 450 miles (724 km). That's because drivers must wind along roads through the Alps mountain range. What are some other features besides mountains that might prevent drivers from traveling in a straight line?

Most maps have a note or symbol that gives the map scale. This tells the relation between sizes on the map and real-world sizes. The map scale may say 1 inch = 1,000 miles. That means every inch on the map equals 1,000 miles on the ground. Some maps have a bar scale, which looks like a ruler. The marks on the bar are labeled with distances, such as 100 kilometers each.

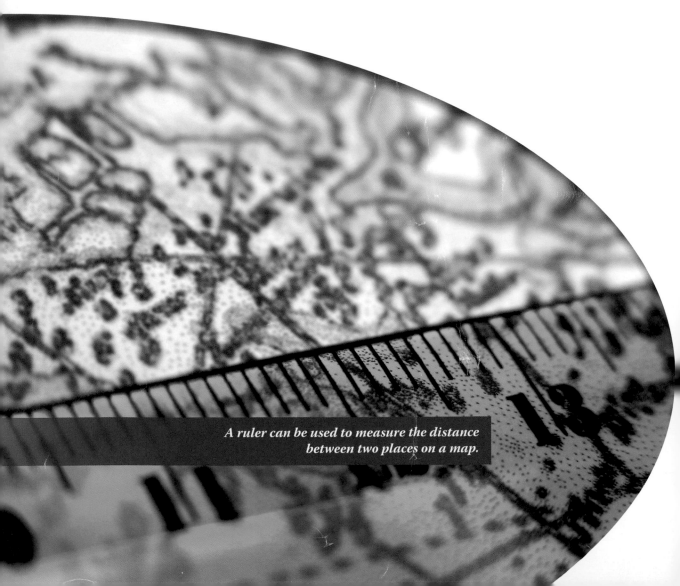

A ruler can be used to measure the distance between two places on a map.

A map scale is often shown as a **ratio**, such as 1:1,000,000. This is read as "one to one million." The scale might be a fraction, such as 1/1,000,000. Or it could be an **equation**, such as 1 = 1,000,000. All these map scales mean the same thing: one unit on the map equals 1,000,000 of the same units on Earth's surface. The units could be inches, centimeters, knuckles, or the distance of one complete pedal stroke on your bike. Any unit can work.

A map scale of 1:63,360 means 1 inch = 63,360 inches. We know that 63,360 inches equals 1 mile. So that map scale is the same as 1 inch = 1 mile. Using this scale, if you drew a map of an area 10 miles wide, your map would be 10 inches wide. For continents, it can be helpful to use a scale of 1:63,360,000. This means that 1 inch on the map equals 63,360,000 inches on the ground, or 1 inch = 1,000 miles.

REAL WORLD MATH CHALLENGE

Suppose you wanted to sail from the southern tip of South America to Antarctica. Your map scale says 1 inch = 500 miles. Measuring on the map, you find that Australia and Antarctica are 1¼ inches apart.

How far would you travel on your trip?

(Turn to page 29 for the answer)

Using this scale, you would find that:

- Asia measures about 5½ inches across.
- Australia is almost 2½ inches wide.
- Africa measures a little more than 5 inches from north to south.
- The distance between South America and Australia is about 7 inches.

Multiply the inch figures by 1,000, and you get a pretty good idea of these distances in miles!

REAL WORLD MATH CHALLENGE

Jared loves hiking, and he can hike 20 miles in a day. His dream is to hike across Australia from east to west. Looking at a map, he measures Australia at 9½ inches across. The map scale says 1 inch = 250 miles. **How many days would Jared's hike take?**

(Turn to page 29 for the answer)

It is a good idea to plan your trip on a map before any outdoor activity such as biking or hiking.

19

CHAPTER FOUR
DO THE MATH: USING LATITUDE AND LONGITUDE

Daniel is lost. He calls home on his cell phone, but he doesn't know where to say he is. Emergency workers can find him, though. His cell phone signal connected with a nearby tower. The search team finds out the tower's exact

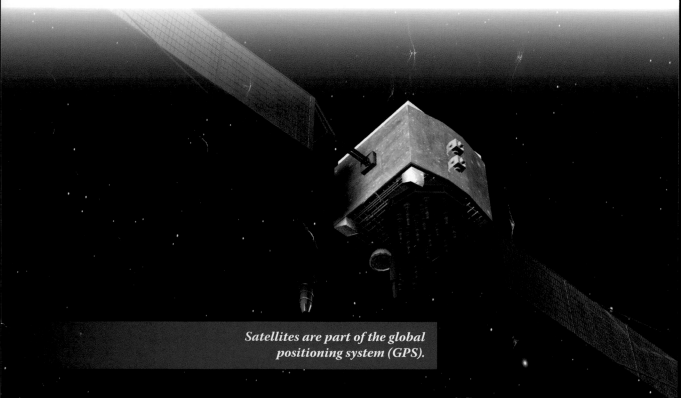

Satellites are part of the global positioning system (GPS).

location. Soon they locate Daniel and get him safely back home again.

How did the searchers locate the cell phone tower? The tower contains a global positioning system (GPS) device. These devices pinpoint an object's exact position on Earth. They use the precise, mathematical language of latitude and longitude. Latitude and longitude are imaginary circles on Earth's surface. They are measured in degrees. A full circle around Earth is made up of 360 degrees (360°).

Lines of latitude circle Earth in an east–west direction. The equator, running around the "fattest" part of Earth, is the largest circle. The other circles become smaller the closer they get to the poles. The equator, at 0° (zero degrees) latitude, is the starting point for measuring latitudes. All points north of 0° are in north latitudes (N). All points south are in south latitudes (S). The North Pole is located at 90° N (90 degrees north) latitude. The South Pole is at 90° S (90 degrees south) latitude. The distance covered by one degree of latitude measures about 69 miles (111 km).

Lines of longitude run north and south. They form circles around Earth that are all the same size. The circles meet each other at the North Pole and South Pole. For longitude, the starting point is the prime meridian, at 0° longitude. Points west of 0° are west longitudes (W), and points to the east are east longitudes (E). East and west meet on the opposite side of Earth from the prime meridian, at the

International Date Line. It is both 180° E and 180° W. The distance between lines of longitude varies, unlike the distance between latitude lines. The equator is the only place where one degree of longitude measures about 69 miles. As Earth curves toward the poles, the length of a degree of longitude gradually shortens until it reaches zero at the poles.

Every location has a latitude number and a longitude number. They identify the east–west and north–south lines that cross there. This set of numbers is called the **coordinates**. For example 19° N, 99° W are the coordinates for a village near Mexico City. That's the capital of Mexico, in North America.

REAL WORLD MATH CHALLENGE

A team of scientists is studying African wildlife. They begin their studies at 12° N and work their way to the equator. Then they turn east and travel another 3 degrees. **How many miles did they travel altogether?**

(Turn to page 29 for the answer)

You can learn a lot about a continent from its coordinates. For example, a place in Africa that's 5° N would be hot because it's close to the equator (0°). The equator is where

The equator is an imaginary line. You can't see it, but many places have markers, such as this one near Kisumu, Kenya, to show where it is.

the Sun's rays hit most directly. So places on or close to the equator are some of the warmest places on Earth. But the tip of South America, at about 55° S, would be quite chilly.

Finding the **antipode** is a fun way to work with coordinates. The antipode is the point on the exact opposite side of Earth from a given location. A line between antipodes would pass right through the center of Earth. To find the antipode of a location, switch the direction of its latitude from N to S, or from S to N. Then subtract the longitude from 180, and switch the E and W directions. For example, 37° S, 175° E is in New Zealand, near Australia. Its antipode is 37° N, 5° W. That's in the European country of Spain. Whenever you stare straight down at the ground, you are looking toward your antipode!

REAL WORLD MATH CHALLENGE

Carlos lives in South America, and his hometown is Río Negro, Argentina. Its coordinates are 40° S, 64° W. He wants to find the antipode of his town. **What are the antipode's coordinates? What city is the antipode of Río Negro? Which continent is it in?** Use a map or globe for help with these questions.

(Turn to page 29 for the answers)

Because so much of Earth is covered by water, most land locations have antipodes in oceans.

CHAPTER FIVE

GETTING A GRIP ON THE CONTINENTS

Which continent has the world's largest sports stadium? Asia! North Korea's Rungnado May Day Stadium seats 150,000 sports fans. That's just one example of a continent's many math facts. Math helps you get a grip on the continents—not just on their geography, but also on their people, natural resources, and fun stuff such as sports.

Mountain climbers use math to measure their climbing abilities. They know that Asia has the highest peaks on Earth, including Mount Everest. At slightly more than 29,000 feet (about 8,840 m), it's the world's tallest mountain. Climbing it

Mount Everest is so high and difficult to climb that reaching the top can take more than 2 months.

is an exciting challenge, but some climbers set an even bigger goal. They aim to scale the Seven Summits—the highest peak on each continent.

Looking at the world community, Asia is home to about 61 percent of all the people on Earth. The two most populated countries in the world, China and India, are in Asia. Another 14 percent of Earth's people live in Africa. Almost 14 percent live in North America and South America combined.

21ST CENTURY CONTENT

Cairo, Egypt, is Africa's largest city. Like all big cities, Cairo has big traffic problems. It can take hours to drive from one side of the city to the other. Cairo also has Africa's only subway system for mass transportation. About 2.7 million people ride it every day. Egypt's transportation minister says the subway cuts down on traffic and decreases air pollution. Can you think of some other benefits that Cairo's subway provides?

What about wealth and poverty around the world? For that we can look at gross domestic product (GDP). That's the value of all goods and services a country produces in a year. Divide that figure by the population, and you get an idea of how much each resident makes in a year (the GDP **per capita**). By this measurement, Africa is deep in poverty. Eighteen of the 20 lowest-ranking countries in GDP per capita for 2005 were in Africa. But Europe is a wealthy continent. Six of the top seven nations in GDP per capita were European countries.

Each continent is distinct in some way. Australia is the world's largest island. Antarctica contains most of the world's ice. Europe uses the most wind-powered energy. South America is tops in **biodiversity**. Its Amazon rain forest has the most plant and animal species anywhere on Earth. Asia grows the most rice, and North America produces the most paper. Africa raises the most cocoa beans, which are made into chocolate. Math is the only way to get a grip on these facts. It helps you make some fun discoveries, too!

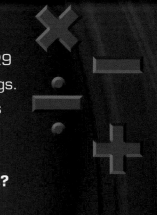

REAL WORLD MATH CHALLENGE

Clare is making her holiday wish list. She wants a $229 iPod, a $198 leather jacket, and a $69 pair of earrings. Meanwhile, Clare's class is studying Africa. She learns that the African country of Burundi had an estimated GDP per capita of $124. **How many years could a Burundian live on the price tag of Clare's wish list?**

(Turn to page 29 for the answer)

REAL WORLD MATH CHALLENGE ANSWERS

Chapter One

Page 7
Five Australias would fit inside Asia.
17 million square miles ÷ 3 million
square miles = 5.67

Chapter Two

Page 12
It is June 25.

December 25 + 6 months = June 25

They will have to wait 9 days for
Independence Day.

From June 25 through June 30
there are 5 days.

30 − 25 = 5

From July 1 to July 4 there are 4 days.

0 + 4 = 4

4 days + 5 days = 9 days

Chapter Three

Page 17
You would travel 625 miles on your
trip.

1¼ = 1.25

1.25 x 500 miles = 625 miles

Page 18
Jared's hike would take about 119
days.

9½ = 9.5

Australia is 2,375 miles across.

9.5 x 250 miles = 2,375 miles

2,375 miles ÷ 20 miles per day =
118.75 = 119 days

Chapter Four

Page 22
The team of scientists traveled
1,035 miles altogether.

12° − 0° = 12°

Remember, degrees of latitude
measure about 69 miles.

12 x 69 miles = 828 miles

Now the scientists are at the equator,
the only place where degrees of
longitude measure about 69 miles.

3 x 69 miles = 207 miles

828 miles + 207 miles = 1,035
miles

Page 24
The antipode is Beijing, China, in
Asia, with coordinates 40° N, 116° E

Latitude: Change S to N; 40° S
becomes 40° N

Longitude: 180° − 64° = 116°;
change W to E; 64° W becomes
116° E

The map shows this is Beijing, China,
in Asia.

Chapter Five

Page 28
A Burundian could live 4 years on
Clare's holiday price tag.

$229 + $198 + $69 = $496

$496 ÷ $124 = 4 years

GLOSSARY

antipode (AN-tih-pohd) the point on the exact opposite side of Earth from another point

biodiversity (bye-oh-duh-VURS-it-ee) the variety of plants and animals within a region

coordinates (coh-OR-duh-nits) numbers and letters indicating a location's latitude and longitude

equation (i-KWAY-zhuhn) a mathematical expression of values that are equal

International Date Line (in-tur-NASH-uh-nuhl DAYT LINE) an imaginary line at 180° longitude where one calendar day changes to the previous or next calendar day

per capita (pur CAP-it-uh) per person

prime meridian (PRIME muh-RID-ee-uhn) an imaginary line passing north and south across the surface of Earth; the zero point from which degrees of longitude are counted

ratio (RAY-shee-oh) a set of numbers that have a mathematical relationship

FOR MORE INFORMATION

BOOKS

McClish, Bruce. *Earth's Continents.* Chicago: Heinemann, 2003.

Sepehri, Sandy. *Continents.* Vero Beach, FL: Rourke Publishing, 2008.

WEB SITES

Continents & Oceans Multiple-Choice Exercise
www.iq.poquoson.org/continentsoceans.html
Test your geography knowledge with this colorful quiz

National Atlas: Latitude and Longitude
www.nationalatlas.gov/articles/mapping/a_latlong.html
Read about how latitude and longitude work

INDEX

ABOUT THE AUTHOR

Ann Heinrichs's travels have taken her to the continents of Asia, Africa, Europe, and North America. She has written more than 230 books for children and young adults on U.S. and world geography, history, and culture. Ann grew up in Fort Smith, Arkansas, and now lives in Chicago, Illinois. When she's not traveling, she enjoys kayaking and bicycling.